ENGINEERING MARVELS

BUILDING

ROUTE 66

KELLY DOUDNA

Consulting Editor, Diane Craig, M.A./Reading Specialist

Super Sandcastle

An Imprint of Abdo Publishing
abdopublishing.com

abdopublishing.com

Published by Abdo Publishing, a division of ABDO, PO Box 398166, Minneapolis, Minnesota 55439. Copyright © 2018 by Abdo Consulting Group, Inc. International copyrights reserved in all countries. No part of this book may be reproduced in any form without written permission from the publisher. Super SandCastle™ is a trademark and logo of Abdo Publishing.

Printed in the United States of America, North Mankato, Minnesota
062017
092017

THIS BOOK CONTAINS
RECYCLED MATERIALS

Editor: Lauren Kukla
Content Developer: Mighty Media, Inc.
Cover and Interior Design and Production: Mighty Media, Inc.
Photo Credits: Cyrus Stevens Avery Papers/Department of Special Collections and Archives/Oklahoma State University—Tulsa Library; James R. Powell Route 66 Collection/Illinois Digital Archives; Lake County Discovery Museum/Illinois Digital Archives; Library of Congress; Marcin Wichary/Wikimedia Commons; Shutterstock

Publisher's Cataloging-in-Publication Data

Names: Doudna, Kelly, author.
Title: Building Route 66 / by Kelly Doudna.
Description: Minneapolis, MN : Abdo Publishing, 2018. | Series: Engineering marvels.
Identifiers: LCCN 2016962879 | ISBN 9781532111082 (lib. bdg.) | ISBN 9781680788938 (ebook)
Subjects: LCSH: Route 66 (Highway)--United States--Juvenile literature. | Roads--Design and construction--Juvenile literature. | Civil engineering—Juvenile literature.
Classification: DDC 625--dc23
LC record available at http://lccn.loc.gov/2016962879

Super SandCastle™ books are created by a team of professional educators, reading specialists, and content developers around five essential components—phonemic awareness, phonics, vocabulary, text comprehension, and fluency—to assist young readers as they develop reading skills and strategies and increase their general knowledge. All books are written, reviewed, and leveled for guided reading, early reading intervention, and Accelerated Reader™ programs for use in shared, guided, and independent reading and writing activities to support a balanced approach to literacy instruction.

CONTENTS

What Is a Road?   4

On the Road   6

Better Highways   8

Choosing a Route   10

Building Begins   12

Paving a Road   14

On the Move   16

A New Era   18

Roads of the World   20

More About Route 66   22

Test Your Knowledge   23

Glossary   24

WHAT IS A ROAD?

Roads are hard, flat surfaces. They have been around for thousands of years. Roads connect houses and towns. Cars, bikes, and people travel down roads. Roads exist all over the world.

Route 66 is a famous road. It was one of the first US Highways. Route 66 was part of a system of roads. It went across the country.

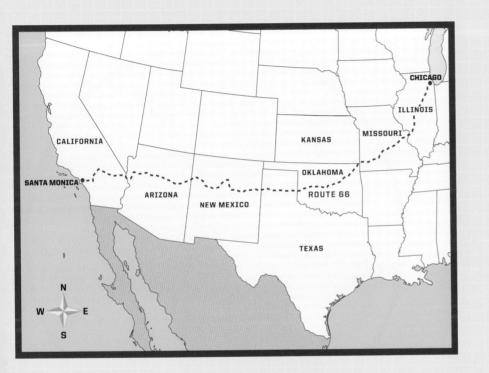

ROUTE 66

LOCATION: United States

ENDPOINTS: Chicago, Illinois, and Santa Monica, California

BUILDING STARTED: 1926

BUILDING COMPLETED: 1938

KEY DEVELOPER: Cyrus Avery

TOTAL LENGTH: 2,451 miles (3,945 km)

ON THE ROAD

Before the early 1900s, travel was hard. Cars were invented in the 1800s. But they cost a lot of money. So people traveled by horse, wagon, or train. The Ford Model T came out in 1908. This car was cheaper than others. More Americans could afford it. But people needed better roads to easily travel long distances.

A Model T

The new Model T cars used auto trails. These were marked roads with names.

BETTER HIGHWAYS

Businessman Cyrus Avery lived in Oklahoma. He knew better roads would help his state. He pushed for a system of national highways. He wanted each one to have a number. The number would tell drivers about the route. One of these new highways would run from Illinois to California. It would be called Route 66.

Route 66 ends in Santa Monica, near Los Angeles, California.

Cyrus Avery

CYRUS AVERY

BORN: 1871, Stevensville, Pennsylvania

DIED: 1963, Los Angeles, California

Cyrus Avery is known as the Father of Route 66. He was part of the group that planned the US highway system. Avery helped come up with the number system for roads. He also helped choose routes. He chose the number for Route 66. Routes going north and south have odd numbers. Routes going east and west have even numbers. Numbers are lower in the eastern and northern parts of the country. They are larger to the west and south.

CHOOSING A ROUTE

Work on the new road began in 1926. But first a route had to be chosen. Route 66 used a **diagonal** route. It mostly ran from east to west. But it also went north to south. The new highway traveled through big cities. It also went through small towns. It connected many communities.

A car drives down Route 66 in Arizona.

BUILDING BEGINS

Route 66 connected existing roads. But workers needed to improve the roads. Route 66 was to be a modern highway. It needed to be fully **paved**. Engineers worked to widen existing roads. They straightened curves. This made Route 66 safer. Signs were placed along the road.

In New Mexico, much of Route 66 was a winding, unpaved road before construction improved it.

PAVING A ROAD

Most of Route 66 was not **paved** in 1926. Some parts were gravel or dirt. Each state was in charge of building its part of the road.

Building a road was hard work. Workers used machinery to create banks. Then they leveled the ground. **Drains** were added. This kept the road from flooding. Finally, the road was paved. Most of Route 66 was paved with concrete and **asphalt**.

A modern road is leveled.

ON THE MOVE

The last part of Route 66 was **paved** in 1938. The new road brought **traffic** to small towns. This helped the towns' businesses. Trucks used the road to carry goods across the country. The US military used it to move supplies. Families took trips along the road. Businesses popped up along Route 66. Restaurants and hotels gave people places to eat and sleep. Gas stations provided fuel. Route 66 became an icon of US **culture**.

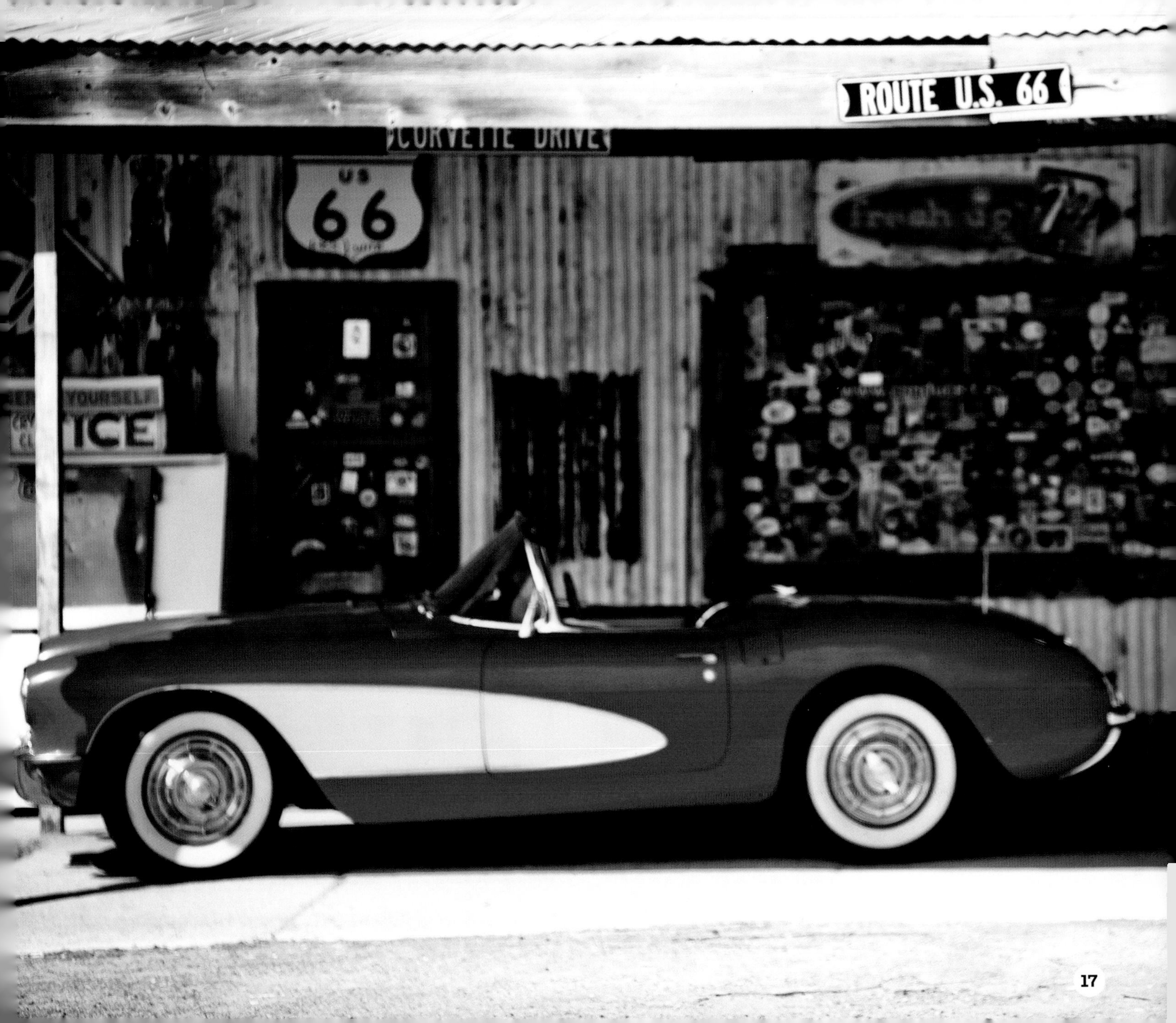
ROUTE U.S. 66
CORVETTE DRIVE
US
66
YOURSELF
ICE

A NEW ERA

By the 1950s, freeways became common. These roads were safer and faster than highways. States no longer kept up Route 66. By 1970, freeways had **replaced** much of the route. In 1985, Route 66 was taken out of service. But many people missed the road. A group formed to **restore** it. You can once again travel parts of Route 66!

A freeway in Washington State

People can still drive parts of Route 66 in New Mexico.

SPEED LIMIT 55

ROADS
OF THE WORLD

SILK ROAD

LOCATION: China, Middle East, Europe

IN USE: 100s BCE to 1600s CE

TOTAL MILEAGE: unknown

BENEFITS: allowed ancient people to travel long distances to share goods and ideas

AUTOBAHN

LOCATION: Germany

IN USE: 1935 to present

TOTAL MILEAGE: about 8,000 miles (13,000 km)

BENEFITS: allows cars to travel across Germany at high speeds

Route 66 is just one of many awesome roads and highways. Check out these other cool roads!

ALASKA HIGHWAY

LOCATION: Canada and Alaska

IN USE: 1948 to present

TOTAL MILEAGE: about 1,500 miles (2,400 km)

BENEFITS: The road was built so the US military could easily move supplies to Alaska. Today it provides a route to Alaska that is open all year.

INTERSTATE HIGHWAY SYSTEM

LOCATION: United States

IN USE: 1956 to present

TOTAL MILEAGE: 46,876 miles (75,440 km)

BENEFITS: Straight roads that go around large cities make traveling long distances easier. Fewer ways to get on the road allows drivers to travel at higher speeds.

MORE ABOUT ROUTE 66

Route 66 crosses through three different **TIME ZONES**.

Route 66 was **NICKNAMED** the Main Street of America.

Route 66 was a popular subject for **SONGS**, **MOVIES**, and **TV SHOWS**.

TEST YOUR KNOWLEDGE

1. Route 66 connected Chicago and New York City. TRUE OR FALSE?

2. What affordable car was released in 1908?

3. In what year did Route 66 become completely **paved**?

THINK ABOUT IT!

Are there any highways near you? Look at a map to find out!

GLOSSARY

asphalt – a black substance that is rolled flat to make roads.

culture – the behavior, beliefs, art, and other products of a particular group of people.

diagonal – running in a slanting direction.

drain – a pipe, ditch, or other structure that water goes through.

pave – to cover a road surface with a hard material.

replace – to take the place of.

restore – to make something like it used to be.

traffic – the cars and trucks driving on streets and highways.